MARY WILSON

NEW POEMS

Mary Wilson

NEW POEMS

Hutchinson of London

Hutchinson & Co. (Publishers) Ltd
3 Fitzroy Square, London W1P 6JD

London Melbourne Sydney Auckland
Wellington Johannesburg and agencies
throughout the world

First published October 1979
Reprinted November 1979

Set in VIP Linotype-Paul Bembo

Printed in Great Britain by
The Anchor Press Ltd and bound by
Wm Brendon & Son Ltd, both of
Tiptree, Essex

British Library CIP data
Wilson, Mary
New poems.
821'.9'14   PR6073.I473

ISBN 0 09 139460 0

Acknowledgements are due to
Sir John Betjeman for permission
to quote from his book, *A Nip in the Air*,
'A Mind's Journey to Diss'
(John Murray, 1974).

To my twin grand-daughters,
Catherine and Jennifer

ACKNOWLEDGEMENTS

Acknowledgements are due to the following, in whose publications individual poems first appeared: Penguin Books Ltd for 'The Opening of Parliament', *The Sunday Times* for 'To Comet Kahoutek', and the *Scillonian Magazine* for the sequence of Scillonian poems.

CONTENTS

PREFACE

I have always believed that a poem should stand by itself, and its meaning be immediately clear to the reader, without the addition of explanations or footnotes; indeed, some poems have charm in their obscurity. However, I feel that it might be of interest if one or two of the poems had a few words of explanation.

Some years ago I said to Sir John Betjeman that I had never re-visited the town of my birth, which I left when I was five years old, and he suggested that we should go to Diss by train, as I said I should like to see if the house where I was born is still in existence. Sir John then wrote a poem called 'A Mind's Journey to Diss'. Soon after our conversation we went to Diss, and I wrote the poem 'Reply to the Laureate'.

The four poems 'In Memoriam John Webster' were written at intervals, following the sudden death in 1974 of this great friend of our family. He was organist at the University Church of St Mary the Virgin, Oxford, for many years, and also organist at University College, Oxford, from 1936 until his death. I knew him from before the war; he played the organ for our wedding and was a constant visitor to our home. He had many friends, and was loved and missed by them and by his pupils and ex-pupils.

I wrote the poem to Nelson because I heard that he was in line for the fashionable 'debunking'. There were many more names I could have included in the poem!

'Speak No Ill' was written following the funeral of the Duke of Windsor in June 1972 at St George's Chapel, Windsor.

As you will see, there is a separate note above the poem about the loss of the *Schiller*. I hope that the other poems are self explanatory.

SCILLONIAN
POEMS

Easter in St Mary's Church

THE church is full of blooms, sweet Island flowers,
And warm Spring sunshine draws their heavy scent;
Anemones and daffodils and hyacinth
Banish the cold austerities of Lent;
And ribboned hats, since summer put away
In maple wardrobes, see the light of day.

Now in the silence, we can hear the sea;
The choir files in, with burnished cross held high;
Pale winter faces lift as we begin the hymn
In worship of the Man who came to die.
The dark is over, and the bright days freed,
And Christ is risen; He is risen indeed!

A Royal Visit

Y<small>EAR</small> after year, men go from here to fight
Or roam the world, but turn to home again,
And sail back up the Road in failing light,
Wiping the sea-salt from their eyes to see
St Mary's twinkling candles in the night.

For this is Merlin-land, and magic lies
(Cast by the wizard over all the West)
Upon these granite rocks, these varying skies,
These blanched-white beaches full of coloured shells,
These lonely islands, racked by sea-birds' cries.

And Major Vigoreux, and Armorel,
Ranulph de Blanchminster, Augustus Smith –
Real or imagined spirits weave their spell;
We hear their voices in the rising storm
Which shakes to wild alarm the warning bell.

And swarthy Charles, fleeing his native land,
Frets in Star Castle, waiting for a ship,
Or strides impatiently across the sand
Looking to France; and one dark night
He hears the muffled oars across the Strand.

Still on the Castle walls the high drums beat;
The last remaining Cavaliers stand firm
'Til overcome by Cromwell's mighty fleet
They march in order down the stony hill,
Bands playing, trumpets blowing, to defeat.

Ghost-haunted in these ancient Isles are we!
But now, another Charles comes sailing in –
Our welcome and belovèd Duke is he,
And from his hidden home upon the hill
He looks through groves of tamarisk to the sea

And sees the waves break on Penninis Head,
Shaking the lighthouse with their thundering roar,
And, turning, finds the sunset sky all red
Behind the Castle. As the storm dies down
The stars are coming out; the ghosts are fled.

My Agapanthus Hedge

Blue, blue, and blue!
But when the sun goes down
Flushing to pink and violet,
Reflecting the evening skies;
Hundreds of heads of blue
Shaking outside my window –
Locks hung with burnished bees
And with creamy butterflies.

Barbecue on Northwethal

THE quay is full of leaping points of light
As the full tide reflects the setting sun;
Our boat strains at the harbour wall
With creaking ropes and bobbing keel –
Let us embark, for soon it will be night.

Now, as we catch the breeze within our sail,
Out from the shallows floats a basking shark;
He swims alongside, keeping pace,
Then near Northwethal, veers away
With undulating form and flicking tail.

Our oars are dipped in silver as we land
With stars of phosphorescence in our wake;
The dog swims, snorting, through the waves
And slips across the slimy stones
To shake himself in frenzy on the sand.

We gather driftwood from the grassy slope
To give a salty sparkle to the flames;
Sea-rocket and sweet samphire grow
Among the rocks, and seaweed lies
Along the tide-mark like a tarry rope.

Fresh mackerel sizzle on the charcoal grill;
On a flat stone which stands within the fire
The kettle sings; hot garlic bread
Is handed round. Drawn from its pool
Within the rocks, the wine is sharp and chill.

Rising like seals up through the tide
Wet-suited divers, dripping crystal drops
Plod up the beach on flippered feet,
To stand around the fire and turn
Their goggled heads slowly from side to side.

And now the lighthouses begin to gleam,
And from its lonely vigil in the West –
The first to greet the sailor home –
Like summer lightning in the sky,
The Bishop Rock shines out its double beam.

We look up to the dark infinity;
The gentle night wind blows the sinking fire
Into a thousand streaming sparks,
And as the Hunter's moon comes up,
We hear the ebbing sighing of the sea.

Commemoration of the Loss of the Liner Schiller, *1875–1975*

On the night of 7th May 1875, the German steamship *Schiller*, bound from New York to Hamburg, foundered on the Retarrier Ledges west of St Agnes, with the loss of 311 lives. The shipwreck was commemorated on 7th May 1975, in the presence of the German Ambassador, the United States Cultural Attaché, and the Chairman of the Council of the Isles of Scilly. Wreaths in the colours of the three countries were thrown upon the sea at the site of the wreck, from the deck of a German rescue ship. Among other commemoration ceremonies, the island children performed a 'Son et Lumière' in Old Town Churchyard.

W E do not come to mourn; the tears
For this sad wreck have all been shed,
And those who wept those far-off tears
For *Schiller*, are themselves long dead.
In reverence to a memory
We cast our wreaths upon the sea.

They float like lilies in the trough,
Until a great wave, breaking high,
Spirals them slowly to the depths,
Through cloudy greenness, 'til they lie
On one torn spar, in rock entrapped,
All barnacled and seaweed-wrapped.

Here, from the grim Retarrier Ledge
Today, the lighthouse seems so near;
Yet on the night the *Schiller* struck –

All through those hours of fog and fear –
The lighthouse keepers heard no cry,
No rocket pierced the stormy sky.

Our medalled coxswain turns the wheel;
Three nations say their last farewell,
And then at speed, the rescue ship
Rides proudly homewards on the swell –
Three nations' voices on her deck;
Three nations' flags salute the wreck.

The dusk comes down on Old Town Church,
And, where a hundred years ago
The island children strewed their flowers,
Once more the childrens' torches glow
To guide us through the falling night;
And in the yellow lantern-light

They act in mime the liner's loss;
We see her strike, we see her sink,
We hear the cries, the muffled gun;
The *Schiller* obelisk glows pink;
And over all, incessantly
We hear the sighing of the sea.

Yes, over all we hear the sea;
We hear its murmuring evermore
In storm, in calm, relentlessly
Ebbing and flowing on the shore.
Encircled in its arms are we –
Our enemy, our friend, the sea.

Spring

Now that the dreary days have run their course
We'll travel down to Scilly once again,
To smell the sweet vanilla scent of gorse,
The froth of garlic in the climbing lane.

The unreaped fields are full of daffodils,
We hear the cuckoo calling clear and plain;
The spring tides surge and seethe across the quay,
And watery sunsets glisten through the rain.

Summer

Two little girls at the edge of the sea
Gaze at the water silently;
With ribbons of seaweed in each hand
They press their feet to the yielding sand.
Scarlet sail on a mizzen mast,
Oyster-catchers scurrying past,
Vapour trails in a brilliant sky,
Shag hanging out their wings to dry,
Fennel and mallow and bittersweet
Growing where pebbles and heather meet;
    This is a picture to hold in mind
    If winter is cold, and the world unkind,
    And summer is only a memory
    Of two little girls at the edge of the sea.

Autumn

W E climb up the path to Penninis Head
To watch the *Scillonian* go by;
But the sea is hidden by drifting mist,
And St Agnes lighthouse floats high
Its base in the fog, and its lantern clear,
Washed by rosy light it is looming near
Like a beacon in the sky.

The spider hangs on its glittering web –
Dew-spangled and evening-spun;
The gulls are wheeling with creaking wings
Clouding the early sun;
The smell of bracken is spicy and sweet;
Water springs from the thrift beneath my feet,
As the whisking rabbits run.

Then in some strange fashion I long to tear
The flesh from my bones, and to pound
The bones into powder, and throw it abroad
On the sea and the rocks and the ground;
To be part of the sea and sand and the grass
And to fly with the soaring gulls as they pass
As they hover and wheel around.

Suddenly, echoing back from the rocks,
We hear the ship's siren blow;
We hear her captain's voice on the bridge,
And the passengers' voices below;

The waves of her wash break upon the shore,
And lost in the mist, she blows once more,
But we do not see her go.

Winter

AND now there comes a file of soft dark days;
The clocks go back, and evening shadows fall
At tea-time; now the boats are all drawn up,
Blunt prows turned seawards, for their overhaul.
When the last lingering visitor has gone
Hotels are shuttered, and the islands turn
In on themselves. The Christmas candles burn
In every window, and the islanders
Too busy through the summer months to greet
Their friends, to hear and to exchange the news,
Stand talking for long minutes in the street
Or in The Mermaid, free from campers now;
And through the shrouding mist and rain they hear
Round Island lighthouse, sounding out the year.
But after Christmas come the winter gales,
When the blown sand and salt spray prick our eyes,
And seas like roaring mountains pitch up stones
Over the driven sea-weed, where it lies
Blown into sodden heaps along the beach;
And fitful gusts of tempest cast the rain
Like water thrown from buckets on the pane.

But sometimes after storm – a day of Spring;
The islands smell of stocks and *soleils d'or*,
Frail tamarisk blooms along the sheltered coves,
And black-backed gulls mince slowly on the shore;
And, snatching back from Winter this one day,
Red sails put out beyond the silent quay,
Past empty moorings to the shining sea.

IN MEMORIAM
JOHN WEBSTER

They Telephoned Me

THEY telephoned to tell me you were dead –
No ageing years for you, no lasting pain,
And I am glad that you have gone ahead
    And I remain.

Yet, having said this, I am desolate;
How could you go away, my dearest friend?
How *could* you go, and never say goodbye
    Before the end?

Of all the evenings when we sat and talked
Nothing remains, no, not one whispered word;
And when I try to recollect your voice,
    No voice is heard.

How many, many times did beauty soar
Towards the chapel-roof at close of day!
But you have shut the organ–loft at last
    And gone your way.

Memorial Concert

JOHN, who loved music with a love so deep
That, hearing some sad cadence, he would weep,
Has gone before us to a quiet sleep.

We miss him sorely, we who stay behind –
Music and friendship in his heart combined
With gentleness; for he was ever kind.

His pupils' notes are muted; but they try
To recollect his high integrity,
His sense of fun, his ready sympathy.

And oh! how much he loved to feel the sun!
To lie 'til the Venetian day was done,
And watch the lights shine on the water, one by one.

So, if he rests on some Elysian shore
Beside a sunlit sea for evermore,
Some echo of our songs to him may soar –

Song may be sweeter in the world above,
But John, we bring this music with our love.

The Passing Storm

I think of you each day with love and pain;
Pain for my loss is like an ebbing tide
Advancing, then receding more and more
As life moves slowly onwards since you died.
   But sometimes a great wave of memory
   Comes crashing through my heart, engulfing me.

I think of you with love for what you were,
And for our long-time friendship, calm and good –
Those rambling conversations late at night,
Nothing withheld, and all things understood.
   Now that the storm is passing, these remain
   With greater love to compensate for pain.

St Cross

IN old St Cross, the blackbirds sing
All day among the cedar trees;
Wild briony and bindweed cling
Around the headstones, and a breeze
Is blowing through the waving grass,
And round the feet of ghosts, who pass

To wander up the curving Street,
Or drift unseen through College Halls,
Hoping some long-lost friend to meet
Among the portraits on the walls –
Until the booming of Great Tom
Summons both ghosts and students home.

Here, Town and Gown lie side by side;
And Maurice Bowra's simple stone
(And laurel wreath from Christmas-tide)
Are just six steps along the path
From where, in polished marble, lie
The station-master's family.

Charles Williams, poet, all alone
Beneath a drooping pure white rose,
'Under the Mercy', says his stone.
The keeper of this quiet plot
Has here, himself laid down to rest
Among the friends whom he loved best.

With downcast eyes, and folded hands
Near Walter Pater's plain stone cross
A terracotta angel stands.
For Kenneth Grahame, near the gate,
No willows weep, but blossom flies
Along the wind to where he lies.

Here are three brothers; crowned with fame
Were two of them – for Academe
Had paid its tribute to their name;
The middle brother, much beloved,
With falling leaves was swept away
In Isis, one October day.

A cry, a splash, an upturned boat –
An empty stream for those who ran
To see the rising bubbles float;
He was a Scholar, just eighteen.
The brothers mourned him through the years
And still remembered him with tears.

And as they sat secure in Hall,
Among the happy voices there
Did one young voice cry over all
'But what of me? What of my life?
Where are the honours for my brow?'
Three brothers rest together, now.

Soldiers and sailors, mountaineers,
Students from far across the world,
Doctors and nurses, engineers

Lie here with dons and scientists
And clergymen, both High and Low;
And over all, the grasses grow.

Sometimes I hear the organ play –
So sweet a sound, to pierce the heart
With echoes of another day;
Remember the Toccata, John,
Pealing in triumph through the night,
The chapel lit by candlelight?

And later, when the crowd had gone,
You played an evening hymn for me,
And in the quiet, still played on.
The shadows shook among the pews,
The candles guttered, one by one.
'Goodnight, dear friend, the concert's done.'

And now your grave is green with moss;
Yew-berries stain the Yorkshire stone
Which marks your place in old St Cross;
The meadow-grass is trodden down
By those who, all the summer through
Come here, to stand and think of you.

Yet clearly now, as one who sees
The image of a memory,
I see you limping through the trees,
Smiling, and shrugging-on your gown
And saying, just beyond full sight,
'Don't fret for me, for I'm *all right*!'

In old St Cross, all through the day,
The floating chimes of Merton clock
Signal the hours and years away;
And grief dulls to acceptance here –
How could I break the spell, and weep
Where Oxford's dreaming children sleep?

Oxford in Wartime

THE silenced bells hang mutely in the towers,
The stained-glass windows have been taken down
To Wales, to shelter underneath the mountains;
And battledress has shouldered-out the gown.
And undergraduates waiting for their call-up,
And feeling restless and dissatisfied
Are fighting with Australians in the Milk Bar;
Yet soon they will be serving side by side.
Flapping in tattered fragments from the billboards,
Torn posters advertise an old Commem,
And some who danced all night have gone for ever –
The Roll of Honour will remember them.
The colleges are full of Civil Servants
Trucking and jiving when the day is done,
And as the evening mists rise over Isis,
The RAF flood in from Abingdon
To the King's Arms, to play bar billiards;
Laughing and talking, flirting, drinking beer
No shadow from the future clouds their faces,
Only a heightened sense of danger near.
The pencil search-lights swing across the darkness,
The bombers throb above through driving rain,
We know that Woolton pie is on the menu
In the new British Restaurant at the Plain.
So tiring of the dreary wartime rations,
To dine at the George Restaurant we go,
Where high above the scene of shabby splendour
The punkas waver slowly to and fro.

The Barrel is rolled out beneath my window,
Deep purple always falls with falling night,
And here, and in the enemy's encampments
Lili Marlène stands by the blacked-out light.
She shines a tissued torch upon her nylons
And ties her hair up in a Victory Roll.
Washing is hanging in the Fellows' Garden,
Evacuees live in the Metropole.
And in the crowded daytime roads of Oxford,
The shifting costumes make a masquerade
As men and women officers, all polished
Mingle with cloaked exquisites from the Slade.
In blue suits and red ties, the walking wounded
Hobble with sticks to help their bandaged feet,
And prisoners-of-war, with yellow circles
On their brown battledress, dig in the street.
And we all live as if there's no tomorrow –
Indeed, for some of us, there will not be –
And 'til the bugle calls us to the conflict
We sit in the Cadena, drinking tea.

Those wartime years have gone, and left no traces,
Fresh tides of youth have swept them all away;
New buildings have arisen by the river,
And there are few who think of yesterday;
Yet sometimes, in the middle of September
Though Spitfires scream no more across the sky,
As dusk comes down, you cannot see the pavement
Where ghosts in blue are walking down the High.

To Nostalgia

You first enthralled me in my early days
Almost before my babyhood was gone;
You set a looking-glass before my gaze
All through my life, to show the light which shone
Brilliant and clear, on days through which I'd dreamed
And scarcely felt life's happiness and pain;
Dim and unreal the present always seemed
Until I saw it mirrored once again.
But now, I try to grasp each passing day,
Yet, as the shadows gather, I suspect
That, in the magic of your spell, I may
Have lived my muddled life in retrospect;
And I am troubled by the fear that I
Like Lot's wife, looking back, may petrify.

A Plea for Heaven

THERE must be somewhere, where the children live
Who die in pain, asking their mothers why?
Some far-off place, untroubled by our tears,
Where they may travel through their stolen years
And lost maturity?

Will those, in battle or in accident
Blasted from life, no time to say a prayer,
Awaken to tranquillity, and find
The suicides, the handicapped and blind
Restored to wholeness there?

And to that country, shall we come at last,
From life, through death, come once again to live
And know at last the reason for our pain,
And those we loved and wounded, see again
And ask them to forgive?

Our childhood images may disappear –
No stern Saint Peter waiting with his keys
To open pearly gates on streets of gold,
No shining angels will their wings unfold
To greet us; none of these,

But such a peace as we have never known,
And such a light as here has never shone
Unless we glimpsed it in the afterglow
On summer Sunday evenings long ago
After the sun had gone.

O Spirit whence we came, it must be so,
It must be so, O God whom we adore!
You would not thrust us into endless sleep,
Into a nothingness so vast, so deep
That we are lost for evermore?

To Comet Kahoutek

AFTER the sun has set, you rise and draw
Your misty train across the winter sky;
Like shepherds long ago, we look in awe
At your cold blaze of soulless majesty.
Forth from the blackest depths of empty night
Through drifts of stars and haloed moons you glide,
And like a moth attracted to your light,
The Space Ship sails upon the evening tide.
Unearthly visitor, you please our eyes
With your rare beauty; but alas we know
That, fixed upon your orbit through the skies,
A thousand thousand years will come and go
Before you circle planet Earth again;
Will anyone be here to track you then?

When the Space Ship Comes

WHEN the travellers come in their ships from outer space
What will they discover – a crowded and starving world
Thronging with skeleton people fighting each other for
food,
With fear and despair and hatred glaring from every face?

Or will they land on an earth wrecked by nuclear war,
Where under the smoking ruins, misshapen children sit
Gazing with empty eyes at the barren and twisted rocks,
And the black and boiling seas as they pound the shrivelled
shore?

Perhaps they will find (for reason at last must prevail),
Lands covered with forest, where free wild animals roam,
Fish spawning again in rivers running limpid and clean,
And a purified ocean, safe for the seal and the whale.

And meadows of flowers opening out to the light –
A daylight unsullied by smoke and poisonous fumes,
And birds nesting high in new-planted clusters of elms,
And unclouded brilliance shining from clear skies at night.

And if this may be, as they look from their strange round
eyes
At this heaven-on-earth, will the visiting space-men see
Man, the destroyer, who came to his senses at last,
Or will he have died away, as each obsolete species dies?

'Let us finish the work which he in his guilt began'
They will say, 'Let us settle here and make this our home,
And learn our lesson from him, from his failures and faults,
And preserve this sweet Paradise to the memory of Man.'

The Flowers of Spring

PRIMROSES, daffodils, jasmine and crocus,
Pale chilly flowers of hesitant Spring,
Gathered with catkins and new-budded branches;
Set in a bowl by the window, they bring
Promise of poppies and daisies and roses –
All the bright tangle of full summer bloom;
Scented like lilies, austere in their beauty,
Lighting with yellow my winter-dark room.

Interlude

Do not go back, dear heart, to where we once were happy –
The grass has grown waist-high, the trees are bare,
The roses have regressed; the strangling bindweed
   Is living there.

How we should love to know again in days of winter,
The summer interlude, the warmth, the sun!
But to recapture moments gone for ever
   Can not be done.

Manic-depressive

TODAY when I awakened to the light,
I knew that this would be a happy day
With no dark dreams remaining from the night,
And no remorse to steal my joy away;

A day in which I feel my spirits soar,
Perceptions heightened, colours bright and clear;
No unknown shadows fall across my floor,
But safety wraps me round and love is near.

*

I should like to dig a deep, dark hole
And lie down in it, as if in my bed,
And to stretch up high and blot out the sky,
As I pull the grasses over my head.

And to have some peace as my heart-beats cease
With the sound of voices fading away;
And to rest at last with my eyes shut fast,
And wait for my body to turn to clay.

The Opening of Parliament

THE Chamber lights are dimmed, then glow again
On ermine robes, Orders of Chivalry,
Dress uniforms, and wigs, and white lawn sleeves,
Long evening gowns, and costly jewellery.

The Cap of Maintenance, the Sword of State
Carried in front of her – with careful tread
Dressed all in white and silver, comes the Queen;
The Imperial Crown is heavy on her head.

Four pages lift and spread the crimson train
As, handed by the Duke, she mounts the throne,
And even in this glittering company,
Admiring eyes are turned to her alone.

Her faithful Commons, summoned by Black Rod,
Come through the corridors and stand to hear;
The Chancellor presents the Gracious Speech;
She reads the legislation for the year

And tells of journeys over land and sea
Through burning heat and cold, that she will make –
So many people pressing near to her
To see her smile; so many hands to shake.

They love her for her wisdom and her pride,
Her friendship and her quiet majesty;
And soon the streets of Britain will be thronged
With crowds rejoicing in her Jubilee.

But as the cool unfaltering voice reads on,
A different picture forms upon the air –
A small quick figure, walking all alone
Across a glen studded with standing deer.

The wind blows freshly from the mountain tops,
Brown water stands in pools among the peat;
She whistles all the Labradors to heel,
The heather crunches stiff beneath her feet.

She sees the swallows wheeling in the sky,
The firs reflected, trembling, in the loch,
The cairns of stone upon the nearer hills,
White flash of waterfalls upon black rock.

She notes a crumbling wall, an open gate,
With countrywoman's eyes she views the scene;
Yet, walking free upon her own estate
Still, in her solitude, she is the Queen.

Speak No Ill

Blackness, and banners, and ancient gold,
And the scraping shuffle of bearers' feet;
Flowers, and tears for a tale that is told,
And choristers' voices, high and sweet;

And a silent, saddened, regretful throng,
And hymns that we had not heart to sing,
Honours, trumpets and pageantry
At the funeral of our uncrowned King.

Even those who cheat and steal and lie
Have someone to speak for them when they die –
A few halting words 'He was always kind',
Or, 'We grieve for those who are left behind'.
But no one that day had a word to say,
We walked to our cars, and we drove away.

Nelson

So Nelson now is due for a debunking!
Why should he stand so proudly in the sky?
Dismiss his virtues, magnify his vices,
Throw down the Column where he stands so high;
Put him with Lawrence, and with Lewis Carroll,
With Barrie, Nurse Cavell and Rupert Brooke
And Florence Nightingale, and Kenneth Grahame;
Yes, denigrate his glory in a book.

We do not want our heroes to be giants,
But look around for ways to make them small,
And having raised their statues and revered them,
We shake the pedestals until they fall,
(All in the name of 'fact' or 're-appraisal'!
Iconoclasm is a better name);
And yet a host as great as Cromwell's army
Will not destroy their honour and their fame.

A Mind's Journey to Diss

Dear Mary,
   Yes, it will be bliss
To go with you by train to Diss,
Your walking shoes upon your feet;
We'll meet, my sweet, at Liverpool Street.
That levellers we may be reckoned
Perhaps we'd better travel second;
Or, lest reporters on us burst,
Perhaps we'd better travel first.
Above the chimney-pots we'll go
Through Stepney, Stratford-atte-Bow
And out to where the Essex marsh
Is filled with houses new and harsh
Till, Witham pass'd, the landscape yields
On left and right to widening fields,
Flint church-towers sparkling in the light,
Black beams and weather-boarding white,
Cricket-bat willows silvery green
And elmy hills with brooks between,
Maltings and saltings, stack and quay
And, somewhere near, the grey North Sea;
Then further gentle undulations
With lonelier and less frequent stations,
Till in the dimmest place of all
The train slows down into a crawl
And stops in silence. . . . Where is this?
Dear Mary Wilson, this is Diss.

John Betjeman

Reply to the Laureate

Dear John,
   Yes, it is perfect bliss
To go with you by train to Diss!
Beneath a soft East Anglian rain
We chug across the ripening plain
Where daisies stand among the hay;
We come to Diss on Market Day,
And cloth-capped farmers sit around,
Their booted feet firm on the ground;
They talk of sheep, the price of corn;
We find the house where I was born –
How small it seems! for memory
Has played its usual trick on me.
The chapel where my father preached
Can now, alas, only be reached
By plunging through the traffic's roar;
We go in by the Gothic door
To meet, within the vestry dim,
An old man who remembers him.
Now, as we stroll beside the Mere,
Reporters suddenly appear;
You draw a crowd of passers-by
Whilst I gaze blandly at the sky;
An oak-beamed refuge then we find,
The scones are good, the waitress kind;
Old ladies, drinking cups of tea,
Discuss their ailments cheerfully.
Across the window-ledge we lean
To look down on the busy scene,

And there, among the booths below,
Fat jolly babies kick and crow
As, wheeled by mothers young and fair,
They jolt around the Market Square.
School-children, dragging tired feet
Trail home along the winding street.
The church clock strikes a mellow chime
Just to remind us of the time;
We climb the hill as daylight fails,
The train comes panting up the rails,
And as the summer dusk comes down,
We travel slowly back to town.
What day could be more sweet than this,
Dear John, the day we came to Diss?

Finsbury Town Hall

I have always loved angels; when I was a child
I knew they were guarding me all through the night,
With their stern noble faces, their big feather wings,
Their solid gold haloes, their garments of light.

Sometimes they would sing, and sometimes they would
    speak
In low, pleasant voices of infinite charm;
And the light of beneficence shone from their brows,
And I knew that with them I should come to no harm.

And tonight we have angels to light us to bed
As the windows grow dark, and the long shadows fall,
Glowing lamps held aloft in their delicate hands –
The elegant angels of Finsbury Town Hall!

The Old Woman of Peckham

My life is made of shadows
Which move across a screen;
Sometimes they bring back memories
Of all the things I've seen.
They showed the War last evening
The mud and the Very lights,
And No Man's Land and the trenches;
I remember the London nights
With the troop trains in the darkness
And the Zeppelins overhead,
The wounded on the stretchers,
And the dreadful lists of dead;
The canteen at Waterloo Station,
And the soldiers, wet and cold –
Hungry for love and excitement;
And one, so handsome and bold,
Held my hand with the teapot in it;
I shall always remember that day,
And he bought me a ring of garnets
Before he went away.
On his next leave we were married,
O I can see us now –
We went up West for our supper,
Then on to 'Chu Chin Chow'.
Thirty-five years we were married,
Snug in this little street,
And even now I listen
For his returning feet.

We had plenty of jokes and laughter –
I don't remember the tears –
With the children growing round us,
Yes, those were happy years.
We both worked hard for our living,
But I really can't complain;
He was with me through the bombing,
And he went without much pain.
The people from the Welfare
Keep on calling on me,
But I won't take anything from them,
Not even a packet of tea;
They always seem to remind me
That I live here all alone,
That my children have married and left me
And my husband is dead and gone.
'Mother, come with us to New Zealand!'
But I didn't want to go,
And (I understood and don't blame them)
They were glad when I said 'No'.
I tried not to show that I'd miss them
When I waved them all away;
I have always lived in London,
And here I mean to stay.
My neighbour fetches my pension
And she shops for this and that;
But I don't let her over the doorstep,
I keep her on the mat;
She's a kindly soul and I'm grateful,
But I wouldn't call her a friend;
I want to be independent
And to be so 'til the end.

Someday soon, I shall need them
(Those people who knock at my door)
When the doctor on the telly
Can ease my pain no more;
But when I have drawn my curtains,
And my fire is burning bright,
I know I'll be able to manage
For just another night.

Nursery Suite

Morning Song

AWAKEN, baby, for the day is dawning!
The sun is shining brightly, to say good-day to you,
The birds are singing sweetly to welcome in the morning,
The flowers are all open, and the sky is blue.

The Rocking-horse

UP and down, up and down,
My rocking-horse is riding to town,
Over the fields and down the street,
Galloping, galloping go his feet;
With his flying mane and his coat of brown,
My rocking-horse is riding to town.

Banbury Cross

MY musical box plays 'Banbury Cross' –
The tune I love best of all,
And Teddy and I ride to Banbury Cross
On my rocking-horse by the wall;
And our shadows go up, and our shadows go down,
And we journey far away;
But we always ride back from Banbury Cross
Before the end of the day.

Pram Ride

WHAT can I see, as I ride in my pram
Under the trees in the Park?
The grass is green, and the lake is blue,
There are roses and daisies and buttercups too,
And children are calling, and little dogs bark
    Under the trees in the Park.

Pigeons and sparrows are flying around
Under the trees in the Park,
There are lots of exciting things to see,
But Mummy is wheeling me home to tea,
And the sun has gone down, and it's growing dark
    Under the trees in the Park.

Bathtime

I love to blow bubbles through my hands,
And pour the water from jug to dish;
And rocking around on the waves that I make
Are my yellow duck and my purple fish.

I kneel up close to the end of the bath
To see my face in the shiny tap,
And the bathroom light looks funny and small.
Then Mummy lifts me on to her lap.

She wraps me up in a fluffy towel
And pats me dry as she holds me tight;
She sings to me as she brushes my hair,
And now I am ready to say good-night.

Good-night

I say good-night as the shadows fall
And my toys are stacked away;
Good-night to my rocking-horse by the wall
And my teddy-bear, tired of play.

My Mummy and Daddy kiss me good-night,
And 'Good-night world!' I say,
And I close my eyes and go to sleep
At the end of my happy day.

Cradle Song

Sleep well, baby, as the dusk is falling,
May God keep you safely through the hours of night;
Our thoughts will be with you, and our love surrounds you
Until it is morning, and the day is bright.

Miss Piggy

CATHERINE has Brownie,
But Miss Piggy belongs to me;
She may not be quick at lessons,
But she's very good company.

I'm afraid she is rather grubby –
She fell under an Oxford bus –
And her satin dress is faded,
But she never makes a fuss.

I tell her all my secrets
When we go for our afternoon rest;
Brownie is pretty and clever
But I love Miss Piggy best.

Brownie

JENNIFER has Miss Piggy,
But Brownie belongs to me;
She can read and swim and crochet,
And make a cake for tea.

Daddy says she's my alter ego
(Whatever those words may mean),
And even when I'm dirty,
She's always tidy and clean.

She tells me wonderful stories
When we go for our afternoon rest;
Miss Piggy is funny and friendly
But I love Brownie best.

Mamzelle

THE Summer Term had just begun;
My desk was warm beneath the sun;
I leaned across the window-ledge
To smell the springing sweet-briar hedge.
The quiet garden seemed to wait;
I heard a footstep by the gate,
Across the grass a shadow fell –
  I looked, and saw Mamzelle.

My mouth is dry as she goes by –
One curving line from foot to thigh –
And, with unEnglish liberty
Her bosom bounces, full and free;
Pale skin, pink lips, a wide blue stare,
Her page-boy fall of silky hair
Swings on her shoulders like a bell;
  O how I love Mamzelle!

She cannot get her idioms right,
She weeps for Paris in the night
Or, in the tension of the Match
She laughs when someone drops a catch!
The other staff are not unkind
But distant; she tries not to mind,
And I would gladly go through Hell
  Just to protect Mamzelle.

On Conversation Walks we go,
I touch her sleeve – she doesn't know;
All summer's beauty round her lies
As '*Parlez français*, girls!' she cries.
I do not smile, I do not talk,
In silence by her side I walk
And hope that no one there can tell
    How much I love Mamzelle.

The sunny days are hurrying past;
Their painful sweetness will not last;
The poppies burn among the hay,
The heartless cuckoo sings all day;
The Home Farm woods are green and cool,
There's laughter from the swimming-pool.
At end-of-term I say farewell
    For ever, to Mamzelle.

Perhaps I shall forget her face,
Her gentleness, her body's grace;
Even her accents, deep and slow,
May be forgotten. And I know
That I, throughout the coming years
May love with joy, may love with tears;
But shall I ever love so well
    As now I love Mamzelle?

An Autumn Rose

This is my last love, and when this has died –
As die, alas! I know it will –
Then I shall seek the warm fireside,
Shall tend the plants along my window-sill,
Read all the books I've hoarded for this day,
Live on my memories; grow old and grey.

But, in this Indian Summer, we have known
A sunset blaze before we part;
Our love is like an autumn rose full-blown
Which opens wide to show its golden heart;
Heavy with fragrance as its petals fall –
Sweetest of all, my love; sweetest of all!

The Coffee Shop

I came in to the coffee shop today
And asked for her – 'Has she gone away?'
'Oh, but she died, didn't you know?
The funeral was two days ago.'

Acquaintances, no more than that;
I had never seen her without her hat;
Yet my tears fall on the plastic top
Of our table in the coffee shop.

I knew nothing about her, or her life;
She wore a ring – was she widow or wife?
I know she has gone – all lives must end;
But, too late I know I have lost a friend.

Sunset

DEAR lost companions, do not forget me
Now that my face is turned to the West;
I see your faces, lit by the sunset,
Friends of my childhood, dearest and best.

So when I step down into the river
And feel your hands outstretched to take mine,
I shall cry, 'Listen, I hear the trumpets!
I see the towers – look how they shine!'

Galilee

Have you come here to find the King?
To feel His glory and His pride,
To see the country where He died?
    Then go to Bethlehem

And from the shepherds' rocky field
Follow with them their joyful search,
To the dark cave beneath the Church
    Of the Nativity.

And on to proud Jerusalem
Where altars glitter in His name,
And priests in splendid robes proclaim
    The lowly Nazarene.

This synagogue is where He taught –
His eager child's precocity
Astonishing His family
    And filling them with awe.

Thence, to Golgotha's sun-baked hill
To pause and hear, across the years
The echo of His mother's tears
    And His despairing cry.

Then take the long and stony road
Past the parched fields beside the way
To find towards the end of day
    The land of Galilee.

And here, the air is fresh and sweet;
Here Jordan is a little stream,
And in the lakeside kibbutzim
   They eat Saint Peter's fish.

An Arab fisherman kneels down
Mending his broken nets by hand
And there beside him in the sand,
   The shining silver draught.

Here you will find no royal Christ,
No humble birth, no shameful death,
Only His spirit, and the breath
   Of His humanity.

A tired, hungry, human Lord
Treading the dust with sandalled feet,
Disciples plucking corn to eat
   Upon the Sabbath day.

He sat at supper with His friends,
Tasting the wine, blessing the bread.
He healed the sick and raised the dead,
   Doing His Father's work.

And when the cooling shadows fall,
Upon the slopes, the cypress trees
Tremble before the evening breeze
   Blown from the Jordan hills;

Half seen, half felt, beside the lake,
Like starlight faintly in the night,
Just out of reach of human sight
   A Presence stands.

Doubts are forgotten, faith is strong
That He was human, yet divine;
The land of Galilee His shrine –
   The dwelling of the King.